REVELATION 2020 SERIES

Psychic

Sight

Learn how to see auras with the naked eye through
Secrets hidden from mankind

JOHNNY FIVE

Edited by Casey Allen

Table of Contents

Chapter 1

Introduction

The intention of this book is to teach you how to start visually seeing auras. It is a fact that human beings can only see a fraction of the total light spectrum. Auras are seen in a higher density. Human beings naturally only see in the third density or 3D for short. In order to see auras, an inner cleansing has to be done so that you can start seeing in a higher density or 4D.

This book is based on the subject of auras but is also deeply tied to other subjects. In order for you to be able to see auras you have to have an understanding of the other relevant subjects mentioned in this book to aid you in awakening a dormant side of your brain to start being able to see the unseen. I will also provide information on these subjects and references from ancient times for credibility because they are all interconnected. Inevitably, learning to see auras will lead you down a path of awakening yourself.

The benefit of awakening yourself will set you on the path to becoming your greatest version. Benefits you can expect to see will be that you become more in tune with the reality around you and above you. We also all have angels or, spiritual guides, assigned to us to accompany us on our journey within this reality. They are not allowed to intervene with our free will, however when we are awakened, we can better communicate with them and become aware of their existence. They can only aid you with your permission. Before I touch on the main subjects, I want to share a story that reveals the inner cleansing I had to go through before I was awakened and able to see in a higher density.

When I became awakened, I started on a path that led me into a deep inner purification of my temple. My temple being my body, mind, soul, and spirit. This cleansing involved a complete detoxification of everything within me and around me. I cleaned up the negative thoughts I had about myself. I swept away the negative family and people within my life. I started spending more money on organic foods instead of material things. I started removing all the subtle poisons we grow up injecting ourselves with into the body. I did these things because I love people and I want to help all my brothers and sisters in this reality through teaching. However I first had to love myself so that I could give others the same love. Like myself, all people have purpose and a personal spiritual journey with unique gifts to contribute to the world. I had to be ready to receive my gift so I could give it away, altruistically.

I use to have an extremely poor fast food diet. I often ate fast food burgers for breakfast, lunch, and dinner. One day after eating a burger, I had to go to the emergency room from pain it caused after consuming it. After this episode, I developed a stomach illness where I would dry heave on the onset of hunger. I have always had a fast metabolism allowing hunger to set in every four to five hours. I carried this illness for three years. This illness was something I became used to. I had every possible medical exam done such as X-ray, CT scan, a scope inserted into me through the mouth (endoscopy). Then a second time, same procedures the second year and doctors still could not figure it out. On the third year, I became awakened and became aware of a group of angels, or guides, assigned to accompany me along my journey. When I would meditate, I would ask them every so often, why am I afflicted with this illness? I am a doer of good, I love people, I help everyone that I can, why am I tormented with this? I remember asking them for the next few months to help rid this illness. With patience and trust in my spirit guides, I knew they would show me what I needed to do at the correct time.

One week I was having random acne breakouts. I have not had acne that bad since I was a teenager. It was not going away, I became aggravated and decided to do some research on how to cure it. Spirit guides have an interesting way for us to intuitively follow in the right direction. My guides led me to a youtube video by an artist named Teal Swan in which she detailed steps about how to cure acne. In one of her steps, she had spoke about doing a liver flush based on Andres Moritz 's liver flush techniques. This part resonated with me so hard it was an unmistakable feeling that I needed to do this and I felt my spirit guides were leading me to do it. When I did the liver flush, I had fifty or so gallstones come out of my liver which had to be repeated until they are all gone in bi-weekly intervals. By the end, I had over 100 gallstones come out. Some as long as a standard sized paper clip and as wide as a quarter.

I would have never watched that video if I had not had an outbreak of acne randomly. I had instant relief from my illness from this flush after suffering for 3 years. My body was speaking to me but I couldn 't hear it. I was not listening. Medical professionals were baffled and could not understand what was causing this and why I showed labs of an above average healthy human being. Prior to this, I never became awakened and asked for the aid from my spirit guides. Those gallstones would have eventually calcified and would have been deposited into my gallbladder later in life and I may of needed a surgery to have the gallbladder removed.

My lesson in listening to my body and being lead intuitively by my spirit guides taught me to listen, be it through meditation or intuition. Loving myself enough to be guided kindly by these spirit guides. Humans lack the understanding that the answers are always around us if we take the time to listen with the intentions set of the answers we seek. The answers come, always if we are willing to be open to receiving the answers.

As we undergo our life cycle, we still have to deal with the past version of ourselves. The first half of our lives we could have had a terrible diet and the second half of our lives a clean diet. We still have to deal with the issues we created in the first half of our life inside the second half at some point. These issues could have been from a poor diet or excessive use of drugs for example. Our guides want to help us although the timing may not be exactly when we want it. You first must ask and then they will orchestrate the path to lead to your true purpose. When you are on the correct path, they will send messages to you through the universal language of numerology to communicate with and remind you that you are on the correct path.

This will involve usually seeing the repeat of a single number three times such as, 111, 222, 333, 444,

555, which all have universal meanings and I will touch up on this on a later chapter. I could not see or understand this until I was on my correct life path. This book is meant to spark an interest that will lead you down a path of self discovery and self awakening beginning on the topic of auras.

Chapter 2

Auras

Have you ever heard the phrase, that person has a bright aura, he has a beautiful aura about him, or her aura illuminated the entire room? Did you know every living thing that exists has an aura? The aura is the dominant chakra energy emitting from an animal or being. We are all energy, everything and everyone. All beings have an energy that emits a color that is a visual representation of many characteristics about ourselves.

These characteristics include our personalities, our dominant strengths, injuries on the body, and the stage of the current development of our soul. When we are able to see the aura in others it can unlock new truths and understandings about our reality and ourselves. A common misconception is that only a few people can see auras, however everyone has access to the ability to see auras. In this book, I am going to expose truths to you based on my personal experiences.

The ability to see the aura is accessible to all human beings once they have an understanding of how it is seen. Awakening your ability to see auras will take time and will not happen overnight. It is like a muscle that has to be cleansed and awakened. Once you have gone through the inner cleansing and exercises provided in this book, you will eventually reach a point where you will see the aura of whoever you encounter without effort. When you discover that you can see auras through the practices and techniques in this book, it will shatter your perception of the reality that we live in. You will start questioning what else have you not been able to see. Seeing auras is only one of many abilities we all have access to.

In the beginning your eyes have not been trained to see auras so you will not see a color outside of white. Initially you will only see a white hue branching out about an inch outwards from the body of whoever you are looking at. The most prominent visibility of the aura will be seen at the shoulder and head levels. Growing up, I could naturally always see auras around people, although I often had a hard time distinguishing the colors. I did not know they were called auras until I started researching what it was I was seeing naturally. I could never see them out in the open or under bright artificial light. In dim settings, I could be speaking with someone and all of a sudden a white hue would appear surrounding them. Naturally, I brushed it off as nothing or visual issues feeling that I needed to be seen by a professional. Do not brush this off as an issue within your eyes or yourself as it is the beginning stages of seeing auras!

As I became older, I started going to different churches on Sunday and noticed usually the pastors and some select individuals always had an extremely bright aura. Even at different churches! Their aura seemed a brighter white or yellow hue more than the average person I saw outside of church. I would approach and speak to them about it and they would have no idea about what I was talking about although they thanked me for mentioning it. It uplifted their spirits to hear me tell them about the light I could see surrounding them.

Approaching the age of an adult, the beginning stages of seeing auras started to progress. One day my brother and I were having a long conversation. As the light became dimmer in the room from the lack of sunlight, I started to notice a blue hue followed behind his head movements where ever he moved. I said to him, I see this blue light following you whenever you move. He was amazed and told my mother and her friend and one by one they each came in the room and asked me to tell them what color of light trailed behind them. I could not quite distinguish everyone at that time.

When I reached the age of 28, I became fed up with the repetitive lifestyle I had and I knew I had a greater purpose that I was not fulfilling. I always had the desire to help others since I was a child and I felt I was not doing my life calling. I became more interested in cleansing my inner body and performing exercises to help train my eyes to see auras. I wanted to train myself to see them more vividly so I could teach others how to see them. I starting reading other books by authors teaching others how to see auras to see if they saw them in a similar fashion as myself.

From reading other books, I realized the way I saw them and the way they were explaining were almost exact. What I noticed is the books I read did not dive deeper into the background of seeing an aura and that cleansing the third eye, or pineal gland, allows you to see them more vividly. At this time I thought one of my missions in this life was that I needed to teach others to see auras and to go deeper than authors before me have. Realizing this may be one of my life missions, I decided I needed to strengthen the ability.

I had several friends I would ask if they would let me practice looking at them behind a white background to help train my eyes. I started to barely see different shades of colors such as green and blue on friends over time which were still very faint to see and I was not even quite sure I saw those colors distinctly. Later on that same year I adopted a plant based diet. One day I went to buy groceries and I had an epiphany to stop eating meat and to adopt a vegan based diet at random. I actually did go into the store to buy meat such as fish and turkey. I assumed my guides were revealing to me what must be done in order to obtain the results I wanted. They knew of my desire to teach others and they wanted to help me accomplish my mission I set out to do. I listened and instead of buying meat, I bought some vegan protein powder and I set out to research how to eat a plant based lifestyle.

Not long after I stopped eating meat and consuming only plant based foods, I started to notice the colors manifesting around people vividly. The colors were no longer questionable of what color the colors were. The colors around people became visible now within 15 seconds allowing me to see the aura around everyone and everything. This is when I discovered the power inside of the plants and that meat prevented me from full access to psychic abilities such as seeing auras. Am I saying you have to adopt a plant based diet to be able to see auras or gain access to psychic abilities? No, however, will it expedite the process? Yes it will.

I was able to see auras before I changed my diet, only the colors were not clear. I tell people all the time that there is power in the plants. I discovered that first hand after seeing the different colors sprouting out from everyone that I looked at only a few days after I stopped consuming meat. During that whole year I still had been eating meat but I was regularly cleansing my pineal gland and meditating here and there. This is how I discovered there was negative energy inside of meat as it was preventing full access to psychic abilities. I started to embrace the positive energy, detoxification, and the many health benefits from a plant based diet. This shift in diet enhanced abilities and awakened dormant abilities within myself.

Chapter 3

How to Practice Seeing Auras

To begin, you will need a friend that will be comfortable allowing you to stare at them so you can exercise the muscle. The aura is not seen with your physical eyes but with your third eye, also known as the pineal gland. This gland is located in the center of the brain next to the pituitary in the frontal lobe where all of our hormones and emotions are stored. In ancient civilizations such as the Egyptians and Sumerians, the third eye was a common known symbol and used regularly.

The third eye is also referenced in the biblical teachings under Jesus and his disciples. Since most people on average have never exercised this muscle in modern days, but have in the past, it is naturally dormant. The pineal gland is also covered by heavy metals so it will need to be decalcified and activated.

Have a friend stand or sit in front of a white background. My friends always happened to have white painted dry walls in their home. Now once your friend is in front of a wall or background a couple feet away from you, pick a focus point whether it is on them or if you want to look past them, as long as you can still see them in your peripheral vision. Also, try not to blink, once you blink you reset your vision which also resets your focus so you will have to keep resetting each time you blink. Try squinting your eyes if you are having trouble staring without blinking. Do this until you are able to maintain a stare to help maintain longer period of focus without blinking.

After about 15-30 seconds of focusing on a point, you will start to see a hue of light appear within your peripheral vision around the person. The aura is not seen with your direct eyesight, it is seen in your peripheral vision. You can have the person sway back and forth while you stay focused on the point and you will see the hue trail behind the movements of the person swaying. It will be seen predominantly above the shoulders and around the head area.

Initially you should not see a color until you have exercised the muscle regularly and decalcified the pineal gland. If you do not see anything at first, do not worry. Keep practicing a few times a week as this will help train and exercise the eye to start seeing energy. If you see a color other than white but like one of the seven colors of the rainbow initially, you may already have a cleansed and activated pineal gland or it just may be a natural sight for you. Then you only need to exercise seeing it through the techniques mentioned. You can also use the same method to see your own aura, you just need a mirror to look at while in front of a white background. You can also look at your hand while it is in front of a white background using the same methods.

Chapter 4

Seven Major Chakras

Before you can understand what each color of the aura means, you must first understand what the aura is linked to. The aura is linked to the seven major chakras. The seven major chakras start at the base of the spine and lead up to above the head.

The first chakra is the root chakra, represented by the color red and is located at the base of the spine. The second chakra is the sacral chakra, represented by the color orange and is located between the base of the spine and the naval. The third chakra is the solar plexus, represented by the color yellow and is located in the stomach region just above the naval. The fourth chakra is the heart chakra, represented by the color green and is located in the chest region. The fifth chakra is the throat chakra, represented by the color blue and located in the throat region. The sixth chakra is the third eye chakra, represented by the indigo color and located at the forehead in the center between and slightly above the eyebrows. The seventh chakra is the crown chakra, represented by the violet color and is located above the head.

You might also notice these seven colors make up the colors of the rainbow. When you understand which each chakra is related to, you can identify what the color reveals about the person whose aura you are able to visually see. In this next section I will explain what characteristics are usually associated with each chakra.

Red Chakra

The red aura represents the root chakra. The root chakra is linked primarily to survival and emotional needs. Characteristics include but not limited to; passion, courage, confidence, and fear.

Orange Chakra

The orange aura represents the sacral chakra. The sacral chakra is primarily linked to sexuality. Characteristics include butt not limited to; creative, fun, freedom, and harmony.

Yellow Chakra

The yellow aura represents the solar plexus chakra. The solar plexus chakra is primarily linked to intelligence and wisdom. Characteristics include but not limited to; optimistic, friendly, joyful, transformation, fulfilled, intelligent, and abundant.

Green Chakra

The green aura represents the heart chakra. The heart chakra is primarily linked to healing, healer, or extreme love for others. Characteristics include but not limited to; unconditional love, compassion, empathetic, sincere, and devoutness.

Blue Chakra

The blue aura represents the throat chakra. The throat chakra is primarily linked to communication. Characteristics of this aura include but not limited to; faith, intuition, gift of gab, leadership, and persuasion.

Indigo Chakra

The indigo aura represents the third eye chakra. The third eye chakra is primarily linked to spirituality and intuition. Characteristics of this aura include but not limited to; imagination, faith, spiritual, intuitive, and knowledgeable.

Violet Chakra

The violet aura represents the crown chakra. The violet chakra is primarily linked to being in complete balance in all of the major chakras (a rare aura to see). Characteristics of this aura include but not limited to; enlightened, fulfilled, awareness, intuitive, complete, whole, spiritual, knowledgeable, and balanced.

Chapter 5

Personal Encounters with Auras

In my personal experience, since I started seeing the colors of auras, I have not yet seen any person with a dominant red or orange chakra. These are usually dominant in animals since they deal with the primitive instincts of emotion, survival, and sexuality at its basic level. In my experience, humans tend to start at the yellow aura and bounce between the third and seventh chakras depending upon which chakra they become most dominant in. The color of your aura can also change, it does not always remain the same color. For example, I have seen a person with a blue aura and a year later they had a yellow aura so they had a major shift in the dominance of their chakra.

People I have encountered with an <u>yellow</u> aura:

Some I have met have an extreme level of intelligence, but reserved, somewhat anti-social, pretty satisfied with the way things are and do not want change.

On the flip side, I have met some that are very social, joyful, vibrant, very friendly, and outgoing. In my experience on average people possessing this aura are usually plugged into this reality. Spending most of their free time watching movies, on social media, playing video games, watching television, getting lost in this reality so to speak and kind of just enjoying the human experience. This is not necessarily a bad thing, it is simply the stage of development their soul is at until it shifts at a later point in their lives. Of all the auras, I see the yellow aura in most of the younger generation of people on average.

People I have encountered with an <u>green</u> aura:

When I have met a person being dominant in the heart chakra, they usually are involved in a profession that is of healing in some way. Some others I have met that were not in a healing profession have an unconditional love for everyone around them. My father for example, has a green aura. Since I was a child, my father had always believed in the power of healing by laying of hands. It was no surprise to me when I first was able to see auras when I looked upon his, it was green. He use to always lay his hands upon or over myself and my brothers as children when we suffered from pain. I had thought nothing of it as a child. It was not until I became older that I realized I had always felt better after he had laid hands over me.

My father studied reiki healing, counseled, and preached. All of which are characteristics of a type of healing. I have a friend that also does reiki healing sessions as a side job, she possesses a green aura also. I have noticed most doctors tend to have a green aura. I had met a man that had a green aura and when I asked him if he worked in a healing profession to my surprise he said he did not. I told him that was unusual because most people I see with a green aura are dominant in the heart chakra and passionately love to heal others. He told me he passionately loved to help others. He said he would do anything to help anyone in need, even give the shirt off his back. I then understood why he emitted a green aura.

People I have encountered with an <u>blue</u> aura:

When I first started seeing auras vividly, I noticed my own aura was blue. Which made sense because the blue aura is the throat chakra which is the dominance of communication. I have always loved communicating with others, writing papers, writing poetry, counseling, public speaking, and have been great at sales through consultation. I am still naturally adept at these characteristics but my aura is now an indigo color which my dominant chakra has shifted to the third eye chakra.

People I have met with a blue aura were quite like myself. Often great public speakers, salesmen, and great communicators. On the flip side, other people with blue aura usually are extremely spiritual individuals. Whether they were religious or not they had a strong faith and strong spiritual practices. Whenever I would communicate with someone with a blue aura, we were often able to speak on a similar level of understanding.

People I have encountered with an <u>indigo</u> aura:

As I mentioned, my aura was once blue and then more recently became indigo. That being said, I am now more dominant in my spirituality and intuition. This book being wrote is a prime example of intuition. I have never wrote a book in my life and when I was meditating one day, my intuition (spiritual guides) revealed me to write books to teach others. I questioned it, why would I write a book on topics there are already books about? Who would read my book when they can get a book from a more renowned person?

My intuition (spiritual guides) led me to realize my exposure of truths and controversial approach to the topics would reach audiences that other books would not. This same intuition throughout my life has guided me. I have always listened and it always led me where I needed to be to learn a lesson or to help a soul. A big portion of my intuition has led me to helping people contemplating suicide throughout my life to intervene and try to prevent them from that path throughout the USA. I was able to help most stray from that path, but some I failed and I blamed myself earlier on. As I became wiser, I realized I was a messenger, or helper, sent to help as many as I could. If I could not help one to continue on to others and not harbor guilt or blame myself.

Another example of a person I have met with an indigo aura is that they were adept at astral projecting, which is the ability to leave the body consciously and travel while sleeping or meditating. And no, it was not Dr. Strange. If my guides want me to teach others how to astral project I will write a separate book teaching others how to perform this technique. Another I have met was adept at being a channeler where messages are able to channel through them from a higher source for the benefit of the person who needed to hear that particular message.

People with this aura tend to have become adept at a particular psychic ability whether they have realized it or not. As with auras, everyone has access to all types of psychic abilities however, you will only become skilled at the one that is your natural ability. As with sports, not everyone is going to be the best boxer, basketball, or football player. However you can understand the sport and play at an amateur level. It is the same concept. You can have access to all psychic abilities but you will only have an affinity to one or a few in which you will be naturally talented at.

People I have encountered with a <u>violet</u> aura:

This is an extremely rare aura to see, as the presence of this aura in a soul means they are dominant and completely balanced in all seven major chakras. I have only seen this in one individual so far. He was acupuncture physician. He and his wife have a business in Tulsa, Oklahoma, where they provide alternative medicine and practices for the public. They have a community sliding scale based set up where the clients only pay what they can afford at minimum $20, up to no cap for an acupuncture session. This man had an extreme passion and love for people and helping others. He was a very intelligent and knowledgeable medical professional. Very personal with all of his clients and had a geniune love for the people. I have never met a medical professional like him.

The aura is the blueprint of ourselves seen in the

physical realm. It is a visible record that reveals to anyone who looks upon you a solid amount of information about you. Even injuries are present in the aura. When you become adept at seeing auras, you can start to notice where a flow of the energy is weak, dim, or not in sync with the rest of the alignment of the aura. This area is usually the result of an injury or a blockage. For example I have been able to look at a person and tell them where they have had injuries before. Injuries such as a broken bone or if they are currently having pain in a spot. I only know because it is present in the offset of flow in the energy emitting from the person.

Chapter 6

Negative Energy Inside Animal Meat

Have you ever made a trip to the local market in the city that you live in and bought free range eggs? The idea behind free range eggs may have impacted you to stray away from the other brand of eggs and spend a little bit more money for the peace of mind. The philosophy behind free range chicken eggs is that essentially a happy chicken produces a better tasting and better quality bi-product. This ideology has deeper roots than the average person may realize. Based on this philosophy it would be logical to assume that good energy produces good energy and that negative energy produces negative energy. Everything that exists is energy, energy cannot be destroyed, it can only be transferred. If a free range chicken produces good energy one could assume that all the other brand of eggs that are not free range produce negative energy.

Animals raised as livestock do not have the best living conditions as their life purpose is purely to be eaten at some point. Livestock on average have poor living conditions and are tortured or mistreated. At the time of their death they become negative energy and that energy is then transferred into the body of the consumers. It is only transferred out through bowel movements. Since we eat on average three times a day, the negative energy resonating in your body never entirely leaves since it continues to go in and come out.

You might ask what does negative energy do for yourself. The answer is simply that it prevents you from becoming the best version of yourself. My personal opinion is that negative energy contributes to causing cancer. Value animals lives as much as your own. They have a consciousness the same as we do and they want to live just like we want to live. Plants do not have a consciousness therefore they do not carry the energy of experiencing fear, death, screaming in pain, being tortured, or being pursued after to be eaten. I did not understand these things until I was able to see energy clearly. When I could start seeing energy regularly it shattered my perspective of the reality that we live in. When you learn to see auras you will see that everything that is living has a color in their energy and that which is inanimate has no color although you will still see its energy.

You will understand that anything that has a soul attached to it will have a color present in their energy showcasing the dominant chakra present in that soul. When you look on an animal you will see its energy and recognize it has a soul attached to its physical body just as we humans do. Animals have a soul, we are no different than them, we are the same, only our experiences of life are different. When you understand this you will respect all life forms as you do yourself. I do not expect anyone to understand this until they have seen energy for the first time as seeing is believing.

If you want to accelerate your progression to see auras I suggest adopting a vegetarian or vegan diet with an emphasis more on the vegan diet. Even if you feel like you could not live without meat you can still possess the ability to use your sixth sense and see auras.

However the negative energy in meat puts a dampened effect on your body preventing you from operating at full capacity so to speak. Many people believe that they can not live a plant based life. I encourage you to do some research on living a plant based lifestyle and try it for one week and see how the shift affects your body. On average, people are unaware of the plant based superfoods such as chia seeds, goji berries, mulberry berries, chlorella, spirulina, moringa powder, and so many more.

People are often afraid that a plant based diet wont carve their hunger like meat will. If you incorporate superfoods into your diet, you can receive plenty of protein that will sustain you throughout the day. As an example, I start the day with a veggie, fruit, nut, and superfood mixed smoothie. This single smoothie sustains my hunger for five hours and gives me plenty of energy to last throughout the day without the need for caffeine. This smoothie blend contains spinach, strawberries, blueberries, a banana, a slice of a pear, goji berries, almonds, a tablespoon of chia seeds, a tablespoon of spirulina, and almond milk. This mix alone fills you with energy, antioxidants, calcium, fiber, and is packed full of protein.

The day the last meal of meat transferred out from my body, I felt a complete shift in my body that was unexplainable. Which was the separation of the negative energy that had been dwelling in me from the meat. Several days later I could visibly see the auras around every single person I came into contact with and to this day there has been no off switch.

Chapter 7

Cleansing the Pineal Gland

Once again, the pineal gland, also referred to as the third eye, is a small gland the shape of a pinecone that is located in the center of each of our brains. This tiny gland is the centerpiece of spirituality and is essentially our sixth sense. It is known to be the doorway to higher levels of consciousness and self awakening. The third eye was used regularly in ancient civilizations. You may be familiar with the Eye of Horus/Ra symbol. This symbol is actually a lateral view of the pineal gland.

In Egyptian lore, Osiris carried a pinecone staff with snakes wrapped around it. Hindu deities, such as Shiva, are also depicted with a third eye on their forehead and is still prevalent in the religion to this day with a red dot in between the eyes representing awakening, enlightenment, and the ability to see beyond. In ancient

Sumerian times, many portrayals of their gods depicted a pinecone in one hand.

The third eye is also referenced throughout the Bible. For example, Matthew 6:22 states, "The eye is the lamp of the body, so if your eye is healthy, your whole body will be full of light." Notice that eye is stated in its singular form and not plural. Jesus had knowledge of the ancients and he passed the knowledge along through his disciples disguised in the Bible so that it would be able to reach future generations without being tampered with.

If it were stated too obviously it would of been removed from the bible like the Book of Enoch and many of the other books that exposed truths to benefit future generations. Ancient civilizations had knowledge of the pineal gland, why is it that in modern times we do not? Higher forces do not want the masses to be awakened or to be able to tap into expanded consciousness and obtain the knowledge of the ancients. They want to essentially keep us working our 9-5 job, keep us in fear, and to keep us under control, never to become our greatest version. The pineal gland has other functions as well such as regulating the internal clock of the body by secreting melatonin to accomplish this. Some symptoms you may encounter while detoxing your pineal gland are headaches, migraines, nausea, or a change in sleep pattern. This rice sized gland also produces DMT, or dimethyltryptamine, a chemical substance that is a powerful hallucinogenic, also referred to as the spirit molecule.

Heavy metal waste products are everywhere in our planet contaminating the environment that we live in. So exposure to these heavy metals are unavoidable. It is in the water we drink from, in the air that we breath, and even day to day products such as deodorant which most contain aluminum. Aluminum can be linked to contributing to the development of Alzheimer disease.

Large traces of it are found in the brain of patients who have the disease. Residue from these heavy metals are deposited in the pineal gland, calcifying it and reducing its effectiveness. Synthetic fluoride from toothpaste and tap water also accumulate in the pineal gland more than anywhere else in the body. Synthetic fluoride also calcifies the pineal gland by creating a hard shell around it. If you live in the USA, chances are there is synthetic fluoride and chlorine in your tap and bathing water. Do you think it is a coincidence that over 70% of the USA 's public water has synthetic fluoride and chlorine in it? It is intentional to keep us dampened, lower our intelligence, and prevent us from accessing the functions of the pineal gland since synthetic fluoride forms a hard crystal shell around the pineal gland. The justification for it is that it gives citizens better dental health. Remember, it is synthetic fluoride, which means it is man made, not natural. Synthetic fluoride is also used in pesticides.

To decalcify the pineal gland you will need to stop consuming water that has fluoride or chlorine in it, do not use toothpaste that has fluoride in it, and do not use deodorant that has aluminum in it. Consume only organic foods. Do not consume anything that has pesticides in it. Organic food is often more expensive, however health is wealth. If you love yourself you will spend more on organic foods than you do clothes, video games, jewelry, technology, app store purchases, and any other material that is meaningless and benefits your health in no way. Consuming seaweed, kelp, kale, and spirulina will remove heavy metals from your pineal gland and decalcify it. Iodine natural binds to heavy metals so iodine droplets is another option for detoxification.

Chapter 8

Activating the Pineal Gland
Disclaimer

Do not activate the third eye if you are not ready to have your perception of this reality broken. If you are comfortable with living how you are now, activating this will could potentially do more harm than good if you are not ready to have the veil of the reality we live in lifted. Activating the third eye will open the doorway to expanded consciousness and you will start to see everything in this reality with 20/20 vision. Opening your third eye may also activate or enhance a natural psychic ability you already have.

    If you are not ready to experience a dramatic awakening shift in your life, do not activate your third eye until you are ready to experience the truths concealed from humankind so that we never become the greatest version of ourselves. The answers are found within ourselves. Once activated, you have access to unlimited information. Everyone has access to all psychic abilities, however you will find that when you are awakened you will have a natural affinity to only one or a few psychic abilities. This has to do with a previously life time where you used this ability or abilities. Once activated there is no going back as all the truths of our reality will unfold before you.

There are different methods for activating the pineal gland once cleansed. There are certain substances you can take to cheat in a way to accelerate the process. I do not recommend that approach as it is not a natural way of awakening so for that reason I will not list them. I found meditation to be the best and most natural way for activation. Meditation is an extremely powerful technique. Meditation is more than just sitting in a cross legged position with your palms out looking for stress relief from your day to day life.

When you meditate correctly your conscious mind hops in the passenger seat and the subconscious mind takes over the driver seat. When you set your intentions in a particular session of what you are wishing to obtain, you are able to gain access to things that otherwise would not be accessible. You may see things, hear things, ideas may be planted in your head, or may hear voices communicating with you, etc.

Like seeing auras, meditating is something that has to be practiced. It is like a muscle that has to be trained. Meditating is different for everyone. Find out what position is best for you. Most people can meditate while in a sitting cross legged position and palms open or flat. For me, I can only meditate efficiently when I am laying down flat on my back or laying down with the back of my neck propped up. That is also a challenge of staying awake as you need to be awake and aware the entire time. Most people do not see or experience anything when they are just beginning to meditate. This is normal, you have to continually train yourself.

In meditation, your intentions must be set while believing in what is trying to be achieved. When beginning meditation, the best times are at night or early mornings after waking up as these times will allow you to quickly get into a relaxed state of mind and expedite the process. However it can be done at any time.

Initially doing some deep breathing (inhaling and hold for a few seconds and exhaling) for a few minutes returning to normal breathing will also expedite the relaxation process. The pineal gland becomes active in darkness just as our physical eyes are active in the light so keep your eyes closed while meditating. Set the mood with intentions with your mind.

Get in a comfortable position and ask for protection for yourself with your mind. It is important to have protection for yourself because when you tap into expanded consciousness, you are exposing yourself to everything beyond and in-between. Only through experience will you learn and until then you will not have a true understanding of what you are doing. It is imperative you do not do anything improper in this ascended state of mind. Always before you start envision protection around yourself with white light and ask your spiritual council to keep you protected. Ask that nothing negative or pessimistic thoughts come to mind while meditating and after thinking believe it is so. State your intentions for your session out loud or in your mind.

Mantras work in this state but do not use past tense or future tense words. Use present tense words such as, I am, or I have. The subconscious mind does not interpret past or future tense so if you speak in those tenses you are working against yourself. Anything you wish to say should be said in a manner that implies you already have or received it. This is how our minds work. The universe will bridge your beliefs into your reality whether positive or negative. This is also known as the Law of Attraction. An example of the use of the Law of Attraction in modern day society is prayer.

The reason prayer works for one and not for another is because one utilizes the Law of Attraction correctly and the other does not. "Therefore I tell you, whatever you ask for in prayer, believe that you have received it, and it will be yours," — Mark 11:24 (New International Bible). Another disguised ancient technique mentioned in the Bible to teach future generations in a way that does not directly expose the technique in an obvious way. When prayer works for one, they pray in present tense. When it works against another, they pray in past or future tense. With this understanding going forward, when you are trying to achieve something, such as opening your third eye, ask in a way that tricks your subconscious mind into believing it is already a reality for you.

Be humble, grateful, and appreciative for your beliefs will manifest into your reality. You can utilize the Law of Attraction like a cheat code used in a video game to get ahead or progress quickly, it is the same concept. You can also use the Law of Attraction to attract abundance into your life (money). Keep in mind that just because you are utilizing the Law of Attraction, that does not mean you can stand around idly and expect results. The mental aspect of the law is only two slices of the pie, your effort and energy is the other eight slices. In other words, I am saying it will not be handed to you on a silver platter, you will have to do the work necessary to acquire what you are manifesting through the Law of Attraction.

Moving forward, envision a white light around you protecting you with your imagination as the mind is very powerful. Keep in mind you can speak to your guides in this state through the use of telepathy (speaking in your mind) or speaking aloud. You can also ask them for protection. Try to keep a clear mind because you have to come to complete nothingness so that you can have a shift in consciousness while still being awake and aware. If any annoying thoughts, music lyrics, or dark thoughts comes to mind, accept it and gently cast it away and keep doing that as they come. Do not allow dark thoughts to irritate or anger you. Accept them for what they are and allow them to be cast aside. If any negative thought comes, continue to gently push them away. Imagine an eye between your eyebrows is opening and a beam of light is protruding out from it. If you need to use a mantra you can make up any mantra that is in present tense and repeat it to cancel out negative thoughts. If a negative thought comes just say your mantra and return to calming and quieting the mind. A mantra is phrased used to aid in manifesting a specific result during meditation. An example, I am grateful my third eye is open.

Furthermore, you will not have to question when it is open, you will know. When you start seeing supernatural things such as, but not limited to; images appearing up before you while your eyes are closed, ideas popping into your head, obtaining random knowledge about something you had no knowledge of, or being communicated with, you will know your third eye is open. Symptoms you may experience are, but not limited to; seeing a red circle that fades over twenty seconds upon waking up from sleep that follows your eye movements and may have geometric shapes rotating inside the circle, seeing energetic signatures of entities upon waking, waking up between 3am-5am every night, seeing orbs appear in and out of your vision during the day, seeing shapes rotate faintly in your vision while eyes are opened or closed, or seeing sacred geometry symbols in dreams or upon waking. The sensitive will open the intuition and will be inclined to follow instincts like never before while having the confidence to trust your instincts (which are your guides aiding you). Try to have thirty minute meditation sessions up to an hour at a time. For some may experience fast results, some may take weeks or months even. It is dependent on how much inner cleansing you have to do.

Bonus Chapter

Numerology

I will not dive too deep in this subject but I wanted to share a little bit of information based on my journey so far in regards to numerology. As I mentioned in the introduction chapter, when you are on the correct path, your spirit council will make it known to you by sending you angel numbers. This is one of the ways they directly communicate with you.

When I began my spiritual journey on my correct path in 2019, I had heard about the angel numbers but I had no idea what they actually were. A friend I was learning some things from had mentioned it to me a few times and sent me some pictures showing the repetitive numbers. Since I never saw them for myself or experienced it, I had no idea what she was talking about or what to even recognize in the pictures. I had jumped onto the correct path about two months prior to her telling me about them. Since I had no idea what she was talking about, it was often a subject we never spoke about much. The universe started pulling me to move to another city and I was hesitant about it. I had a job opportunity come up in Conway, Arkansas. I felt like I needed to go but I still contemplated between staying in a comfortable spot or packing up everything and moving to a city where I knew no one. During the transition of my contemplation, I was helping one of my friends in their print marketing company. They print thousands of papers a day for different jobs. One day I was picking up a stack at random and the bottom of the page number said 555. I thought nothing of it until a few minutes later I picked up another stack at random and it also had 555 on it.

Mind you this machine is sending out papers rapidly and I was grabbing and bundling them as quickly as I could at random. I started thinking to myself if this was not a coincidence, I would pick up another stack at random and it would have 555 on it. After a few minutes, I went to grab another stack and I grabbed another 555 paper and it blew my mind. It was such a supernatural phenomenon that I had never witnessed before and I became frightened at first. This is the point where I started to see the angel numbers. I will list the general meanings of the angel numbers on another page. The angel number 555 has several general meanings. It typically means that a major change is coming your way, trust your instincts, continue on the path you are currently on, your works are being aided by divine beings, or taking the risk presented in front of you as you will be rewarded for it. The same day after I was blown away by 555, it happened again on 888 and I thought no way it could happen again. Sure enough I picked up a second and third 888 stack and I had to sit down after that as I was mind blown. The angel number 888 represents financial and material abundance coming into your life.

This phenomenon is already happening to thousands of people across the world. Only a minority of the total population, but it is occurring to thousands already across the world, not only myself. Once you start seeing the numbers, you will not stop seeing them.

You will see them everyday as long as you are on the correct life path. You will randomly feel the urge to look at a certain object or time and you will see the message they have prepared for you. You may go to pick up the phone randomly and see the time and it will be one of the triple angel numbers. You may even see it on a license plate or a sign while driving. It will be a supernatural tugging to make sure you see the message. When you see these numbers, there is no mistaking that you are being watched, guided, and aided by a council of your angels. Speak to them as you would a friend, appreciate them, and thank them.

The number you will likely see secondary will be your life path number which I will explain how to calculate that. My life path is 11, which is a master number. The master number 11 means Master Intuitive. So in addition to the angel numbers, what I see often secondary in addition to the triple repetitive numbers is the number 11.

For example, I will often be tugged or led to see these times to remind me of my life path, 2:11, 3:11, 4:11, 5:11, etc. I was even placed into an apartment that has the number 11 as the apartment number. The numbers never lie. I often get randomly placed into hotel suites that also have 11 when traveling. I also work in a building that has 11 as its suite number. We all are always being communicated with, we just have to pay attention.

111:
Spiritual awakening and enlightenment.

222:
Miracles, opportunities, and to have faith.

333:
Reassurance that you have been heard by your spirit council and to have faith that what you asked for is coming to you.

444:
This represents encouragement, to not be depressed. You are supposed to experience whatever you are experiencing. Continue on the path. Trust in yourself.

555:

A major change or shift is about to happen in your life. Have faith and continue forward. Allow this shift to happen as it is for your benefit.

666:

This is mistaken to be a bad number in modern days. It is not. It means you are currently out of balance. You may be afraid of losing material attachments, or obsessed with something or someone. Seeing this number means you need to restore balance back into your life. Do not let the things or people around you bring you down.

777:

You are serving your life purpose.

888:

Abundance is headed your way. Being rewarded for past karma. Good deeds are getting ready to be repaid to you.

999:

Something is completed or coming to an end soon.

1010:

You are in a time of spiritual awakening and development. Continue to keep your thoughts, focus, and intentions on your life purpose.

1111:

The number of ascended masters such as Buddha or Jesus Christ. Reminder you came here to make Earth a better place for future generations. A opportunity portal has opened for up for you. Connection to higher realms that can help you reach your highest potential and manifest your desires.

1212:

Relates to relationships, build bonds with the like minded people around you, surround yourself with others that can influence your future and help you accomplish your soul missions.

Life Path Number

Your life path number is who you are and what your natural talent is. If you have a job utilizing your life path, you will be the best at it. It also is an identical match to your character and personality. As I said before, the numbers do not lie. When you understand your life path, you will understand the moment you were born your identity was already laid out. It is up to you to wake up at some point in your life and recognize this and start walking in alignment with your destiny.

You could hypothetically go your entire life never to complete your souls purpose in this life time due to never awakening yourself. When we incarnate here, we agree to adhere to the rules of this reality. Which is not remembering anything prior to incarnating here as it would take away from the experience. It is our duty to wake up on our own at some point in our lives and get on the path to accomplishing what we set out to do prior to incarnation. We choose our life path prior to incarnating. We change paths every incarnation.

How to calculate your life path number

You take your birth date and add each group numbers together individually and you add the total amount together then keep adding until you get to a single digit except in the case where the total equals 11, 22, or 33. These numbers are known as the Master Numbers. When you are using 11 or 22 in a day or month, you do not add them individually, you keep them as 11 and 22. So all of November dates you will add 11 to the total instead of $1 + 1 = 2$.

A few examples.

Being born on December 26th, 1995 is life path 8.

$1 + 2 = 3$	Month
$2 + 6 = 8$	Day
$1 + 9 + 9 + 5 = 24$ Year	
$3 + 8 + 24 = 35$	Month + Day + Year
$3 + 5 = 8$	Life Path

Being born on November 22nd, 2011.

$11 = 11$

$22 = 22$

$2 + 0 + 1 + 1 = 4$

$11 + 22 + 4 = 37$

$3 + 7 = 10$

$1 + 0 =$ life path 1

The date of my birth is May, 31, 1991 and I have the life path of a Master Intuitive.

$0 + 5 = 5$

$3 + 1 = 4$

$1 + 9 + 9 + 1 = 20$

$5 + 4 + 20 = 29$

$2 + 9 = 11$

Since my life path equals a master number, you do not add $1 + 1$ totaling 2.

Albert Einstein was born on March 14, 1879 and he had the life path number 33 which is a Master Teacher.

$0 + 3 = 3$

$1 + 4 = 5$

$1 + 8 + 7 + 9 = 25$

$3 + 5 + 25 = 33$

$33 =$ life path

Since this totals a master number, you do not add the 3 + 3 together equaling 6.

Life Path 1:

Leader, boss, captain, opens doors, paves way

Life Path 2:

Peacemaker, intervener, mediator, diplomat

Life Path 3:

Communicator, expressor

Life Path 4:

Teacher, builder

Life Path 5:

Freedom, change seeker, adventurer

Life Path 6:

Caretaker, nurturer, provider, manager

Life Path 7:

Seeker, searcher of truth, the thinker, introvert, loner

Life Path 8:

Powerhouse, inspirator, dynamic force, wrecking ball

Life Path 9:

Humanitarian

Life Path 11:

Master Intuitive

Life path 22:

Master Builder

Life Path 33:

Master Teacher

JOHNNY FIVE

Conclusion

In conclusion, it is my mission to reveal to humankind that we all have a purpose and the journey to figuring out that purpose has to be found within. Everyone has access to abilities that are commonly thought to only be available to a select few if only you go into the temple that is your body and seek them out. The treasure is within you, do not seek wealth outside when the wealth is within you already.

Knowledge is wealth. Once you tap into the knowledge that is hidden within your temple, you will have all the wealth in the world. That wealth is freedom, expanded consciousness, and transcendence. I hope this book will help you to do much more than see energy. I hope it will spark an interest in you to start or advance your spiritual journey. It is not an intention of mine to offend anyone who reads this book. I wish to aid in the transcendence of humankind. The body is the temple and the third eye is the throne. You only need to go inside and sit upon it to obtain the greatest gift. That gift is becoming your greatest version. I wish love, peace, and abundance upon all of you.

About the Author

Johnny is a 29-year-old Creek Native American from Tulsa, Oklahoma. He currently lives in Conway, Arkansas providing spiritual and metaphysical services for his local community. Since a young age, Johnny has been able to see things within our reality that are naturally invisible to us. He has been able to see and speak with spirits and entities throughout his life. Initially, he believed to be plagued with this connection as being able to have these abilities made it challenging to function in a society such as how we live in today's age that does not recognize on a global scale that beings other than humans exist. Having no one to share this information without being accused of being crazy or having a medical disorder, he tuned them out earlier in his life until the visits became less frequent and began to cease. Even though he toned them out, the spirits still aided him from behind the scenes, guiding and teaching him along the way. When he became older, he started to return to his spiritual roots and the spirits reappeared as if they had never left but only had remained hidden from view. Johnny believes, as he has been led to believe by his spiritual council outside of the physical realm, that he was a Native American shaman in a past life and he has been called again to continue his work in this life by providing healing, spiritual services, protection, and revelation about the unseen forces that exist within our reality to his community and citizens that he comes into contact with. Johnny can provide some services from a distance via phone or webcam. He mentions that with permission from the client he can provide a few of his services to clients anywhere in the world as their permission allows him to connect to their energy and the spirits that preside over them. Johnny extends an invitation to connect with him regarding any questions or concerns you might have related to spiritual matters or about his books. Contact him on Facebook or Instagram, links provided.

www.Facebook.com/Johnny52020
www.Instagram.com/J5_2020